Contents

Introduction

If you are wild about learning and wild about animals – this book is for you!

It will take you on a wild adventure, where you will practise key spelling skills and explore the amazing world of animals along the way.

Each English topic is introduced in a clear and simple way with lots of interesting activities to complete so that you can practise what you have learned.

Alongside every English topic you will discover fascinating facts about the animals which live in the world's polar regions. Life in the Arctic and Antarctic is difficult. It is extremely cold and conditions are harsh, but many animals have adapted to survive here.

When you have completed each topic, record the animals that you have seen and the skills that you have learned in the explorer's logbook on pages 44–45.

Good luck, explorer!

Suffixes *able* and *ably*

Suffixes are one or more letters that are added to a root word, changing or adding to its meaning.

You can add **able** to a **root word** to make an adjective. If you add **able** to a word ending in **ce** or **ge**, you need to keep the **e** when you add the **able** suffix:

change ⟶ *change<u>able</u>*

Another suffix is **ably**. When added to a root word, this suffix makes the word an adverb:

notable ⟶ *nota<u>bly</u>*

FACT FILE

Animal:	Killer whale or orca
Habitat:	All the world's oceans
Weight:	5443 kg
Lifespan:	50 to 80 years
Diet:	Seals, sea lions and even whales

Task 1 Add the suffix **able** to these root words to make a new word, then use your word in a sentence.

a depend: _____

_____

b comfort: _____

_____

c allow: _____

_____

d accept: _____

_____

Task 2

Remember the rule about words ending in **e** before you add **able** to these root words.

a change _____

b notice _____

c love _____

d desire _____

e breathe _____

Task 3

Add the suffix **ably** to the following root words.

a consider _____

b understand _____

c advise _____

d reason _____

e rely _____

WILD FACT

Killer whales work together in pods to hunt for their prey. Shoals of fish are first stunned by a slap from these massive creatures' tails before being devoured!

WILD FACT

Killer whales, send sound waves – echolocation – that travel underwater, giving them information about the location, size and shape of their prey.

Exploring Further ...

Add a suitable suffix to the words in the box and use the new word to complete the sentences.

replace	rely	consider	understand

a Killer whales are _____ bigger than most other ocean creatures.

b _____, most species of fish are afraid of these predators.

c Echolocation is a _____ way for killer whales to determine the location, size and shape of their prey.

d We need to ensure that killer whales do not become endangered because they are not _____.

Now swim to pages 44–45 to record what you have learned in your explorer's logbook

3

Suffixes *ible* and *ibly*

You can add **ible** to a **root word** to make an adjective. Some words that take **ible** as their **suffix** do not have an obvious root.

*poss**ible***   *poss**ibly***

Put your investigator's hat on! Have you ever heard of a 'poss'?

The suffix **ibly** can be added to a root word to make an adverb.

Task 1

Change these root words using the suffix ible to make adjectives.

a   horror   _____

b   terror   _____

c   sense   _____

d   reverse   _____

e   audio   _____

WILD FACT

Humpback whales sing to each other for hours on end using moans, grunts and wails, which travel for great distances under water.

WILD FACT

The humpback's dorsal fin sits on a huge hump on its back, hence its name.

FACT FILE

Animal:	Humpback whale
Habitat:	Oceans and seas throughout the world
Weight:	Approx. 36 000 kg
Lifespan:	45 to 80 years
Diet:	Krill, plankton and small fish

Task 2

Add the suffix **ibly** to make adverbs from these words.

a sense _____

b force _____

c vision _____

d divide _____

e irresistible _____

Task 3

Write sentences using some of the adjectives and adverbs you made in Tasks 1 and 2.

a _____

_____

b _____

_____

c _____

_____

d _____

_____

e _____

_____

Exploring Further ...

Can you find words ending in **ible** and **ibly** from these anagrams? The first letter of the word is in bold.

CABLES ICES _____ BIG YEL**L** _____

BY IN LES**S** _____ **R**EPLY SOBS IN _____

BELLS OIL **C**AP _____

Now splash to pages 44–45 to record what you have learned in your explorer's logbook

Suffixes *cial* and *tial*

The **suffixes** **cial** and **tial** are both pronounced 'shul'. The suffix **cial** is mainly used after a vowel and **tial** after a consonant.

offi<u>cial</u>   *essen<u>tial</u>*

There are some exceptions to the rule (of course!), such as *finan<u>cial</u>* and *ini<u>tial</u>*.

Task 1   Solve the anagrams to make words that end in **cial**.

a also ic _____

b alligac _____

c alf aic _____

d feel can ibi _____

Task 2   Complete these sentences using an appropriate **cial** word from Task 1.

a Belugas swim in the _____ seas of the Arctic.

b Stan thinks that whales are very _____ creatures.

c Exercising every day is very _____ to your health.

d Beluga whales communicate using _____ expressions.

Choose a word from the box then add the correct suffix to complete the sentences.

commerce   essence   office   torrent   influence   residence

a _____ statistics show that whale numbers are growing.

b At the end of our school year, we are going on a _____ trip for a week.

c It is _____ that belugas are not over-hunted.

d The television _____ advertised a whale protection charity.

e The WWF is _____ in protecting endangered animals.

f The whale-watchers struggled in the _____ rain.

WILD FACT

The beluga's skin was used in the manufacture of the first bulletproof vests. Their thick skin and a 10–15 cm layer of blubber mean that they are adapted to freezing water.

WILD FACT

The name 'beluga' comes from the Russian word *bielo*, which means 'white'. Belugas are born dark grey and it can take up to 8 years for them to turn completely white.

Exploring Further ...

Find words ending in **cial** and **tial** hidden in the word-search grid. The first letter of each word is red to help you.

I	T	A	P	S	L	A	I	C	A	R
A	R	L	R	K	O	S	N	D	E	A
R	A	A	E	O	M	C	F	S	A	C
T	O	I	M	A	R	T	I	A	L	I
I	A	T	A	C	A	D	N	A	D	L
F	S	A	R	I	E	D	A	H	L	A
I	B	P	O	N	L	E	N	P	E	I
C	U	S	T	A	G	O	C	E	I	C
I	N	I	T	I	A	L	I	H	C	A
A	A	R	E	S	H	C	A	W	N	L
L	A	I	T	R	A	P	L	P	U	G

residential
partial
financial
artificial
social
initial
glacial
spatial
martial
racial

Now glide to pages 44–45 to record what you have learned in your explorer's logbook

Suffixes *cious* or *tious?*

Some words end in the **suffixes cious** or **tious**. Both are pronounced as 'shus'. The rule is that if the root word ends in **ce**, the suffix **cious** is used:

gra*ce* ——→ gra*cious*

There are exceptions to the rule: *conscience*, which becomes *conscientious*.

If the word ends in **tion**, then the suffix **tious** is added:

cau*tion* ——→ cau*tious*

FACT FILE

Animal: Sea lion
Habitat: All oceans and seas except the northern Atlantic
Weight: Up to 1000 kg
Lifespan: 20 to 30 years
Diet: Fish, squid and shellfish

Task 1	Turn these nouns into adjectives ending in **cious**. Remember the rule about root words ending in **ce**.

a vice _____

b malice _____

c space _____

d office _____

e avarice _____

f grace _____

g suspicion _____

h ferocity _____

Task 2

Use the suffix **tious** to turn these nouns into adjectives.

a ambition _____

b infection _____

c nutrition _____

d conscience _____

e fiction _____

Task 3

Using a dictionary to help you, join these **cious** and **tious** words to their correct definitions.

a fractious   self-important

b conscious   greedy

c pretentious   aware

d tenacious   unruly, irritable

e avaricious   determined

Exploring Further ...

Use the words in Tasks 2 and 3 to complete these sentences.

a Many sea lions swallow stones, which do not form part of a _____ diet.

b As sea lions are an endangered species, we should be _____ of what we do in their environment.

c The sea lion expert, who was very _____, became head of the wildlife charity.

d He talked a great deal about sea lions, but he sounded rather _____.

e The children were tired and _____ after a long day at the wildlife park.

Now dive to pages 44–45 to record what you have learned in your explorer's logbook

Suffixes ence and ance

FACT FILE

Animal: Leopard seal
Habitat: Antarctica
Weight: Up to 400 kg
Lifespan: 12 to 15 years
Diet: Fish, squid, smaller seals and penguins

The suffixes **ence** and **ance** are used to make nouns. It is easy to misspell words with these suffixes because the sound they make at the end is not emphasised – or stressed – so both of these final syllables sound very similar. There are some general rules but, as always, there are some exceptions too!

Use the suffix **ance** if a related word has an '**ay**' sound in the right position:

observ<u>a</u>tion ——→ observ<u>ance</u>

If there is a related word with an '**eh**' sound in the right position, use **ence**:

confi<u>d</u>ent ——→ confi<u>dence</u>

If a noun is formed from a verb that ends in **y**, **ure** or **ear**, then the ending of the noun will be **ance**:

disapp<u>ear</u> ——→ disapp<u>earance</u>

If a noun is formed from a verb ending in **ere** or **er**, then the ending will be **ence**:

interf<u>ere</u> ——→ interf<u>erence</u>

WILD FACT

Leopard seals' front flippers are long, with claws along the edge. They use these flippers with their hind flippers to swim.

| **Task 1** | Choose either the suffix **ence** or **ance** to change these words into abstract nouns. |

a hesitate _____

b tolerate _____

c obedient _____

d innocent _____

e dominate _____

f defend _____

Task 2 Change these verbs into nouns. Take care with words ending in **y** or **e**.

a clear _____

b reassure _____

c comply _____

d endure _____

e apply _____

f guide _____

Task 3 Change these words into nouns.

a interfere _____

b prefer _____

c adhere _____

d infer _____

e transfer _____

f confer _____

WILD FACT

Your fate is sealed! Leopard seals are fierce predators with powerful jaws and long teeth. They attack and kill small seals and penguins.

WILD FACT

'Ere 'ere! Leopard seals have no ears, but their senses of smell and sight are very well-developed. This helps to make them excellent hunters of prey.

Exploring Further ...

Use either **ence** or **ance** to turn these words into abstract nouns, using a dictionary to help you.

a persevere _____

b absent _____

c rely _____

d insist _____

e exist _____

Now slide to pages 44–45 to record what you have learned in your explorer's logbook

Suffixes *ent* and *ant*

The suffixes **ent** and **ant** are used to form nouns and adjectives from verbs. The noun tends to relate to a person who does something:

inform ⟶ inform*ant*

Some words follow the rule that an **'ay'** sound in the right position means that an **ant** suffix is used.

hesitate ⟶ hesit*ant*

Words with an **'eh'** sound use an **ent** suffix.

descend ⟶ desc*ent*

Two related suffixes are **ency** and **ancy**, which follow the same general rules.

Following a hard **'c'** sound, the suffix **ancy** is used.

vacant ⟶ vac*ancy*

Following a soft **'c'** or **'g'** sound, **ency** is used.

decent ⟶ dec*ency*   agent ⟶ ag*ency*

Of course, there are exceptions to these rules.

FACT FILE

Animal:	Harp seal
Habitat:	North Atlantic and Arctic Oceans
Weight:	Up to 180 kg
Lifespan:	20 years
Diet:	Fish and crustaceans

Task 1 — Create nouns from the verbs by adding the suffix **ent** or **ant**.

a contest _____

b assist _____

c reside _____

d account _____

e apply _____

Task 2

Change these words into adjectives.

a tolerate _____

b independence _____

c hesitation _____

d obedience _____

Task 3

Use the rules to change these words by adding the suffixes **ent, ant** or **ency**.

a ascend _____

b fluent _____

c dominate _____

Task 4

Choose the appropriate suffix to change these words into nouns.

a transparent _____

b pregnant _____

c truant _____

d buoyant _____

Exploring Further ...

Are these words nouns or adjectives?
Write **N** for a noun and **A** for an adjective.

a independence ☐

b evident ☐

c pregnancy ☐

d efficiency ☐

e radiant ☐

Now slip to pages 44–45 to record what you have learned in your explorer's logbook

Words ending *fer*

When you add a **suffix** to a word ending in **fer**, you have to say the word aloud to identify where the stress falls so you can decide whether you need to double the **r**.

If the syllable **fer** is still stressed after the suffix is added, the **r** is doubled:

refer ⟶ referral

If **fer** is *not* stressed after the addition of the suffix, then the **r** is not doubled:

refer ⟶ reference

FACT FILE

Animal: Walrus
Habitat: Arctic Ocean
Weight: Up to 2000 kg
Lifespan: Up to 40 years
Diet: Shellfish

WILD FACT

Despite being very slow on land because of their big, clumsy bodies, walruses are fast and strong in the water. They can dive down to around 90 metres for their favourite food: clams.

Task 1 Complete the table by adding appropriate suffixes to each word.

	-ed	-ing	-ence
refer			
prefer			
infer			
transfer			

Task 2

Add the correct suffix to each of the words in Task 1 to complete these sentences.

a The sick walrus was _____ to a specialist veterinary clinic.

b The _____ had been made by a local research scientist.

c The scientist's _____ had been to bring a specialist vet to the walrus.

d In his report, the vet _____ that the walrus's ill health was down to pollution.

Task 3

These words are spelled incorrectly. Can you correct them?

a deferrence _____

b suffrance _____

c offring _____

d profering _____

e diffrence _____

f conference _____

Exploring Further ...

Use a dictionary to find out the meanings of the words in Task 3.

a _____

b _____

c _____

d _____

e _____

f _____

Now roll to pages 44–45 to record what you have learned in your explorer's logbook

15

Using hyphens

Hyphens can join a **prefix** to a **root word**, particularly if the prefix ends in a vowel and the root word also begins with one:

co-ordinate

Hyphens can also join two or more words together:

face-to-face

If you leave out the hyphen, the word might have a completely different meaning:

re-form – to form again and *reform* – to improve

Hyphens can also be used to join two words to show a combined meaning:

good-hearted

Task 1

For each root word, use an appropriate prefix from the box to make a new word.

co-	de-	re-

a operate _____

b sort _____

c icer _____

d enter _____

e own _____

f cover _____

g worker _____

h sent _____

Task 2

Join these words to their most appropriate partner, then write the hyphenated word.

a self   tempered   _____

b sugar   mouthed   _____

c bad   time   _____

d part   employed   _____

e open   haired   _____

f blonde   free   _____

Task 3

Create hyphenated words using the words in the box, then use these hyphenated words in the sentences.

thinking	custom	up	quick	to	built	date

a The Arctic researchers were operating from a _____ observation station.

b An _____ report shows that Arctic wolves are only in danger from humans.

c The _____ Arctic wolves surrounded the musk oxen and attacked.

Exploring Further ...

Complete the table with words that could go before the hyphens in these combined adjectives.

	-	prone
	-	mad
	-	skinned
	-	thinking

Now run to pages 44–45 to record what you have learned in your explorer's logbook

Rules: *i before e*

FACT FILE

Animal: Wolverine
Habitat: Arctic regions of Europe, Asia and North America
Weight: Up to 18kg
Lifespan: 7 to 12 years
Diet: Plants, berries, rabbits and rodent.

The rule **i before e except after c** is more easily remembered if you can memorise it as a rhyme. You won't be surprised to hear that there are some exceptions to this rule!

Where the sound after a soft **c** is 'ee', the spelling is **ei**, like *conceit*.

Some words have an **ei** spelling despite not coming after a soft **c**; they have an 'ay' sound, like *eight*. Others have an **ei** spelling but an 'ee' sound, like *weird*.

Task 1   Unscramble the bold words in these sentences, then write the words on the lines.

a The wolverines gathered in a **ifled** of snow and ice.

_____

b A **cipee** of caribou meat fell from the wolverine's mouth.

_____

c Wolverine babies, called kits, are full of **smifchei**. _____

d We had a **freib** glimpse of the wolverine kits. _____

Task 2   Unscramble the words in the box and complete the sentences.

ceedevir   cefrie   vilebee   digweeh

a Yesterday I _____ a postcard with a picture of a wolverine.

b The wolverine looked very _____.

c I _____ that the wolverine eats animals as well as plants.

d My suitcase _____ too much for me to be able to carry it.

Write the **ei** words that the following definitions are describing.

a We use scales to measure this. _____

b Our blood runs through these. _____

c Found in coffee and tea. _____

d Someone who lives next door. _____

e The noise a horse makes. _____

f Free time. _____

g It comes after seventh. _____

WILD FACT

Wolverines are the largest members of the weasel family. Although only around 100 cm in length, they will attack prey as large as caribou – at least three times their size!

WILD FACT

Wolverines can travel as much as 24 km in one day in search of food. One male was reported to have covered more than 800 km in 42 days.

Exploring Further ...

Complete this crossword. All the answers contain either **ie** or **ei**.

Across

3. Grabbed

4. Found in meat, fish and eggs

6. What we measure to see how tall we are

7. To form an idea

Down

1. A creamy brown colour

2. Strange/odd

3. Enough

5. Protect from

Now climb to pages 44–45 to record what you have learned in your explorer's logbook

Ough letter strings

The letter string **ough** is one of the trickiest to spell in English. It can be used to spell a few different sounds.

Say this sentence out loud:

*Alth**ough** the lemming th**ough**t the weather was r**ough**, he was t**ough** and pl**ough**ed on despite a bad c**ough**.*

FACT FILE

Animal: Lemming
Habitat: In or near the Arctic
Weight: Up to 110g
Lifespan: 2 years
Diet: Leaves, grasses, roots and bulbs

Task 1   The bold words have been spelled as they sound. Using the **ough** letter string, write the correct spellings.

a Despite the **drowt**, the lemming managed to survive. _____

b He burrowed **throo** the deep snow. _____

c Finally he **brawt** some seeds up to the surface. _____

d However, there wasn't **enuf** to go round them all. _____

e So he had another **thuru** search. _____

Task 2

These pairs of words are pronounced the same but the spelling can be confusing. Create a sentence for each word to show you know their meanings.

a threw _____

through _____

b doe _____

dough _____

c bough _____

bow _____

Task 3

List six words that contain the letter string **ough** where it is pronounced 'aw'.

a _____

b _____

c _____

d _____

e _____

f _____

WILD FACT

You may have heard that lemmings commit mass suicide by throwing themselves off cliffs when they migrate but (fortunately for the lemmings) this is a myth!

Exploring Further ...

What's the word? Unravel the anagrams to spell **ough** words.

a ugh or bo _____

b thug ohr _____

c dug ho _____

d gut ho _____

Now burrow to pages 44–45 to record what you have learned in your explorer's logbook

Silent letters

Some letters that were sounded hundreds of years ago are no longer sounded today. The letters often remain in the words, though. For example, *knight* used to be pronounced with an initial hard 'k' sound. The spellings of these words may not make a lot of sense, but they just have to be learned!

Task 1 Underline the silent letters in these words.

a gnarl

b psychology

c Wednesday

d wreckage

e succumb

f knitting

Task 2 Write five words which start with a silent k.

a _____

b _____

c _____

d _____

e _____

Task 3 Write five words which start with a silent w.

a _____

b _____

c _____

d _____

e _____

Task 4

Use the words from the box to complete the sentences below.

| wrestle | island | scientists | silhouette | numb |

a Because of global warming, polar bears can sometimes get stuck on an _____ of ice.

b My fingers were _____ because it was so cold.

c Polar bears have been known to _____ with whales before killing and eating them.

d The bear's _____ is very distinctive with its large posterior, long neck and pointed nose.

e _____ predict that, unless we take action to stop climate change, we will lose our polar bears.

WILD FACT

After a hearty feeding spree in the autumn, the pregnant female builds her den by digging two chambers in the snow. She will give birth to up to three cubs in November or December.

WILD FACT

Polar bears prey on ringed seals basking on the ice. The bear crawls forward slowly then freezes in place when the seal raises its head. A bit like the game 'Mr Wolf'!

Exploring Further ...

Each of the red letters is silent in these words. Can you find all four in each row? Some of the letters are given to help you.

G: s _ _ n,   h _ _ h,   l _ _ _ t,   r _ _ _ n

D: h _ _ d _ er _ _ _ _ f,   a _ j _ _ t,   e _ _ e,   b _ _ _ _ e

N: a _ _ _ _ n,   c _ l _ _ n,   c _ _ d _ _ n,   s _ _ _ _ n

P: c _ _ _ s,   c _ _ p,   r _ _ _ b _ _ _ y,   c _ _ b _ _ _ d

Now pad to pages 44–45 to record what you have learned in your explorer's logbook

Homophones and homonyms

Homophones are words that **sound the same** or very similar (pronunciation) but have **different spellings** (usually) and **different meanings**.

For example, the following two words have the same sound, but different meanings and spelling:

hair   *hare*

Homonyms are two words that have the **same sound and spelling**, but **different meanings**:

bear (the animal)   *bear* (to carry)

Sometimes there are more than two words in a group, such as 'bear' in the example above, and:

bare (naked)   *bear* (to put up with)

I couldn't bear to be bare like that bear!

Task 1   Write a matching homophone to the following words.

a whale _____

b cereal _____

c morning _____

d right _____

e seen _____

f pain _____

Task 2   Unravel the anagrams then pair with a homophone; for some you will find more than one!

a doat _____

b fit pro _____

c rawn _____

d saire _____

e spoer _____

f elfx _____

Task 3   There's something wrong with some of the words in each of these sentences. Rewrite the sentences using the correct spelling of the 'wrong' word.

a We watched as the Arctic hair eight the twigs and routes of the tree.

_____

b A mail Arctic hair likes to catch the attention of the female bye boxing his competitors.

_____

_____

c A fully-groan Arctic hair can bee 5.5 kg in wait.

_____

d After the attack by the bare, the Arctic hair was left with bleeding pause.

_____

e It didn't seam fare that the Arctic hair had to dye.

_____

WILD FACT

Arctic hares have long, muscular hind legs and feet, allowing them to move quickly over snow and ice at speeds of up to 64 km an hour!

WILD FACT

Put your paws up! During the mating season, Arctic hares stand on their back legs and box and scratch each other to impress females.

Exploring Further ...

Create your own homophone and homonym game! Write pairs of homophones and homonyms on separate pieces of paper. Turn them all upside down and, with at least one more person, turn over two at a time. This game will test your memory skills! The winner is the person who has collected the most pairs of homophones and homonyms.

Now hop to pages 44–45 to record what you have learned in your explorer's logbook

Super-tricky homophones

Some **homophones** are super tricky because they have the **same root** (not route!) and a **similar meaning** but a difference of maybe one letter. Other words are 'near homophones' – they don't sound exactly the same but similar enough that people often misspell them, like *affect*, which is usually a verb, and *effect*, which is usually a noun. Sometimes the slight difference in sound is down to different accents.

FACT FILE

Animal: Ermine
Habitat: Woods and fields of Europe, Asia and North America
Weight: Up to 250 g
Lifespan: 2 to 3 years
Diet: Rodents, frogs and fish

WILD FACT

Ermine don't have very good eyesight although, as nocturnal creatures, they see a lot better at night. They have white fur in the winter for camouflage.

Task 1   **Circle the correct word in the sentences below. Use a dictionary to help you.**

a The weather can <u>affect / effect</u> the food chain in polar regions.

b The <u>practice / practise</u> of keeping records of ermine populations has helped researchers.

c After some good <u>advise / advice</u>, the researchers were able to pinpoint the problem.

d Arctic veterinary specialists have to hold an official <u>license / licence</u> in some areas.

Circle the correct 'near homophones' in these sentences.

a The Arctic hare ran father / farther than the ermine.

b As guessed / guest speaker at the convention, the professor was the ermine expert.

c The professor complemented / complimented the student on his excellent report.

Task 3 Create one sentence containing these pairs of homophones to show the difference in meaning.

a lead   led

_____

b passed   past

_____

c aloud   allowed

_____

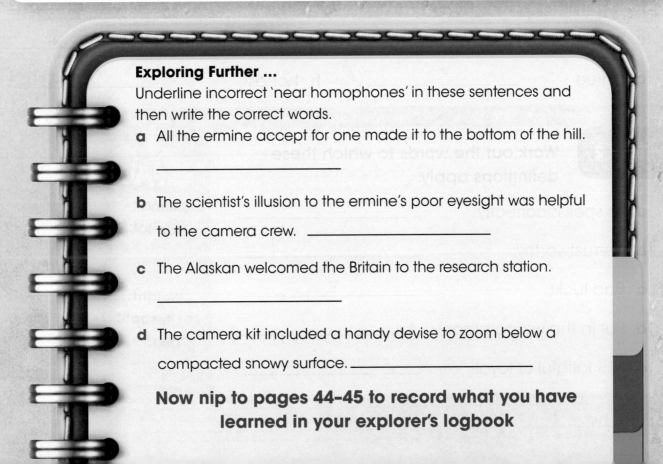

Exploring Further ...

Underline incorrect 'near homophones' in these sentences and then write the correct words.

a All the ermine accept for one made it to the bottom of the hill.

_____

b The scientist's illusion to the ermine's poor eyesight was helpful to the camera crew. _____

c The Alaskan welcomed the Britain to the research station.

_____

d The camera kit included a handy devise to zoom below a compacted snowy surface. _____

Now nip to pages 44–45 to record what you have learned in your explorer's logbook

Prefixes *dis* and *mis*

The prefixes **dis** and **mis** usually give the root word a negative meaning.

tasteful ⟶ *distasteful*

There are no rules about these prefixes: you just have to learn them!

Task 1
Add either the prefix **dis** or **mis** to the following words to change their meaning. Use a dictionary to help you.

a appoint _____

b represent _____

c figure _____

d agree _____

e understanding _____

f guided _____

g connect _____

h honest _____

Task 2
Work out the words to which these definitions apply.

a To spell incorrectly: _____

b Untrustworthy: _____

c Bad luck: _____

d Put in the wrong place: _____

e Not faithful or loyal: _____

FACT FILE

Animal: Musk ox
Habitat: The tundra of Canada and Greenland
Weight: Up to 360 kg
Lifespan: 12 to 20 years
Diet: Plants, grasses and mosses

Task 3

Choose either the prefix **dis** or **mis** to join to the root words in the box, then use the words to complete the sentences.

| agree led similar laid appointed |

a Don't be _____ by the musk ox – he might be a herbivore but he will fight to the death!

b Researchers _____ about the environmental issues affecting the musk ox population.

c The guide was _____ not to see the musk oxen.

d The scientist had _____ his binoculars.

e With their huge size and long, thick hair, Arctic oxen are not _____ to buffalo.

WILD FACT

The good old days … musk oxen date back thousands of years to the ice age, when they shared the Earth with woolly mammoths and sabre-toothed tigers.

WILD FACT

Musk oxen get their name from the strong odour given off by males during the mating season. They urinate to mark their territory, and the odour gets trapped in their long, thick coats.

Exploring Further …

Write a short passage about musk oxen using four of the words below. You can change the tense to suit your writing.

discover   display   disagree   disappear   disease   dislike

_____

_____

_____

_____

Now charge to pages 44–45 to record what you have learned in your explorer's logbook

Prefixes *im* and *in*

Another prefix that gives a negative meaning is **in**. If the root word starts with **m** or **p**, use **im** instead.

definite ⟶ *in*definite
valid ⟶ *in*valid

mature ⟶ *im*mature
perfect ⟶ *im*perfect

Task 1

Add the correct prefix to these words to give the opposite meaning.

a polite _____

b mobile _____

c decent _____

d capable _____

e probable _____

f offensive _____

Task 2

Unravel the anagrams to find words starting with **in** or **im**.

a nail by iti _____

b mineral ops _____

c stem mid o _____

d vain lid _____

e some blip is _____

WILD FACT

The Arctic fox is adapted to temperatures as low as minus 50°C with its insulating fur and increased blood circulation to its feet, which stop its paws freezing to the ice.

Task 3 Choose an appropriate word from the box, add the correct prefix and complete these sentences.

| complete   patient   accurate   adequate   mobile |

a The cameraman got _____ waiting for the Arctic foxes to emerge from their dens.

b Without its insulating fur, the Arctic fox's skin would be _____ against the frigid temperatures.

c The scientific data about the impact of global warming was felt to be

_____.

d After the attack by the wolf, the Arctic fox was temporarily _____.

e The internet fact file on the Arctic fox was proved to be _____.

WILD FACT

Winter white! The colour of the Arctic fox's fur depends on the season. In winter, it is white so that they blend in with the snow, while in the summer it is brown.

WILD FACT

The Arctic fox has exceptionally good hearing. They have wide, front-facing ears which allow them to locate the precise position of their prey beneath the snow.

Exploring Further ...

Write sentences using the following **in** and **im** words in context.

improper   incorrect   inability   immeasurable

_____

_____

_____

_____

_____

_____

Now trot to pages 44–45 to record what you have learned in your explorer's logbook

31

Prefixes *il* and *ir*

The prefixes **il** and **ir** also give the root word an opposite meaning. The rule is to use **il** before words starting with **l** and **ir** before words starting with **r**.

legal → **il**legal

replaceable → **ir**replaceable

Task 1 Add the correct prefix to the following words to make the opposite meaning.

a literate _____

b regular _____

c legitimate _____

d legible _____

e reparable _____

f reversible _____

g relevant _____

FACT FILE

Animal: Reindeer or caribou

Habitat: The Arctic and northern regions of North America and Eurasia

Weight: Up to 320 kg

Lifespan: 15 to 20 years

Diet: Lichens, grasses, moss and leaves

Task 2 Choose the appropriate prefix to add to the words from the box, then complete these sentences. Use each word once only.

legal   responsible   logical   respective

a Some _____ people discard waste products that are potentially dangerous to wild animals.

b The research student made some quite _____ comments about reindeer dietary needs.

c It is _____ to dump waste anywhere that could endanger animals.

d Reindeer manage to stay warm, _____ of the cold, due to their many adaptations.

WILD FACT

Reindeer have a strong sense of smell which helps them to locate the lichen that they eat, even to a depth of 60 cm beneath the snow.

Task 3 The following are definitions for words starting with **il** or **ir**. Use a dictionary to help you find the right words for the meanings.

a Not permitted or allowed. _____

b Ignorant about books; uneducated. _____

c Showing lack of reason or understanding. _____

d Not connected or important. _____

WILD FACT

Unlike other deer, both male and female reindeer have antlers. Male reindeer shed their antlers each winter and grow a new set.

Exploring Further ...

Unravel the anagrams to find words starting with **il** or **ir**.

a sister liberi _____

b litle ateri _____

c rail ration _____

d glaci olli _____

Now click to pages 44–45 to record what you have learned in your explorer's logbook

Making nouns

FACT FILE

Animal:	Snowy owl
Habitat:	The Arctic tundra
Weight:	Up to 3 kg
Lifespan:	9 years
Diet:	Lemmings, rabbits, birds and fish

Sometimes we can make a **noun** from a verb by adding a **suffix**.

For example:
read ⟶ reader
run ⟶ runner

Task 1 Use the suffixes **ing, er, or** and **tion** to turn these verb infinitives into related nouns. You may use more than one appropriate suffix.

a to situate _____

b to build _____

c to educate _____

d to create _____

e to garden _____

f to suggest _____

g to invent _____

h to invite _____

WILD FACT

Female snowy owls sit on their eggs until they hatch, after about a month. The male feeds her while she keeps the eggs warm and safe. If food is scarce, she won't lay any eggs at all until the supply improves.

Task 2

Turn the bold verb infinitives in the brackets into appropriate nouns, remembering the need for subject–verb agreement.

a The (**to attack**) swooped down on its prey _____

b The snowy owl has a keen sense of (**to hear**) _____

c The zoologist was an (**to advise**) to the filmmakers _____

d Snowy owls are great (**to hunt**) of lemmings. _____

Task 3

Add the correct suffix from the box to each word and make as many related nouns as you can, from each one.

tion ment al ance ant ive ity

a assist _____

_____

b relate _____

_____

c govern _____

_____

d publicise _____

_____

WILD FACT

Hide 'n' seek! Snowy owls have excellent eyesight but, to capture prey buried under snow, they rely on their keen sense of hearing. Unlike most other owls, they hunt during the day as well as at night.

Exploring Further ...
Add the missing related words to complete the table.

Infinitive	Noun (1)	Noun (2)
	policing	
		investigation
To cook		
		nurse
	predator	

Now swoop to pages 44–45 to record what you have learned in your explorer's logbook

Making verbs

Sometimes we can make a **verb** from a noun by adding a suffix to the root word. Examples are **ise**, **ify**, **ate** and **en**.

Task 1 Use the suffixes **ise, ify, ate** or **en** to turn these nouns into verbs.

a identity _____

b indication _____

c magnification _____

d length _____

e priority _____

Task 2 Make infinitive verbs from each of these words.

a apology _____

b advertisement _____

c sympathy _____

d improvisation _____

e classification _____

f modification _____

g peace _____

h horror _____

FACT FILE

Animal: Penguin

Habitat: Antarctica, Australia, New Zealand, Chile and South Africa

Weight: Up to 45 kg

Lifespan: Up to 20 years

Diet: Fish, squid and crustaceans

36

Task 3

Choose an appropriate suffix to change the words in the box to suitable verbs for the following sentences.

| clarification apology hesitation custom strength |

a The oil company had to _____ for the oil spill.

b The scientist wanted to _____ which type of penguin they had seen.

c He tried to _____ his bag using pictures of penguins.

d We should _____ the protection of these delightful birds.

e I would not _____ to go on a trip to Antarctica.

WILD FACT

The Emperor penguin is the tallest of the species, reaching a height of 120 cm.

WILD FACT

The Chinstrap penguin is so-called because of the thin black stripe under its beak, which makes it appear to be wearing a helmet.

Exploring Further ...

Turn these word into verbs using **ise**, **ify**, **ate** or **en**, then write a sentence using them in context. See if you can make them about penguins!

a hyphen _____

_____

b fossil _____

_____

c solid _____

_____

d broad _____

_____

Now swim to pages 44–45 to record what you have learned in your explorer's logbook

Changing *y* to *i*

To add suffixes to **adjectives** ending in **y** there are some rules to follow. Have a look at these:

happy

happiness   happier   happiest   happily

Think what the rule is. What would you do if you wanted to add the suffixes **ing** or **ed** to a **verb** ending in **y**?

WILD FACT

Puffins' beaks are backward-pointing, which allows them to store rows of fish in their mouths without swallowing them. They have been known to hold as many as 62!

Task 1   Add the suffixes **ness, er, est** and **ly** to these adjectives.

a lazy   _____ _____ _____ _____

b naughty _____ _____ _____ _____

c pretty   _____ _____ _____ _____

d silly   _____ _____ _____ _____

e stealthy _____ _____ _____ _____

Task 2 — Add the suffixes **ing** and **ed** to each of these verbs.

a multiply _____ _____

b vary _____ _____

c certify _____ _____

d accompany _____ _____

e obey _____ _____

Task 3 — Make the appropriate changes to the words in the box and then complete these sentences.

| **justify   jolly   vary   identify** |

a Puffins are the _____ of birds; they really enjoy 'clowning about'!

b Their plumage takes on a _____ of colours, depending on the season.

c The researcher struggled to read the _____ tag on the puffin he was tracking.

d There was no _____ for building yet another Arctic research station.

Exploring Further ...

Find a pair of connected words for each of these words.

apply _____ _____

satisfy _____ _____

rely _____ _____

Now fly to pages 44–45 to record what you have learned in your explorer's logbook

Latin and Greek

Some suffixes and prefixes have their origins in Greek or Latin, like **bi** meaning two, **super** meaning greater and **tele** meaning far off. If you learn their meaning, it will help you to work out the meaning of the whole word.

FACT FILE

Animal: Albatross
Habitat: The northern Pacific and the Southern Ocean
Weight: 10 kg
Lifespan: Up to 50 years
Diet: Fish, squid, krill and crabs

WILD FACT

Albatrosses have the largest wingspans of any bird in the world, reaching up to an incredible 3.5 metres.

WILD FACT

Nineteen of the 21 species of albatross are threatened with extinction. The main cause is longline fishing vessels. Incredibly, albatross are dying at a rate of around one every five minutes.

Task 1

These words begin with the prefix **auto**. Write a definition for each word and then decide on a meaning for 'auto'.

a automobile _____

b autobiography _____

c autograph _____

auto means: _____

Task 2   These words start with the prefix **bi**. Write a sentence containing each word.

a bicycle   _____

b binoculars _____

c biannual   _____

d bilingual   _____

Task 3   Find three other words that have each of the underlined prefixes or suffixes. Use a dictionary to help you.

a <u>trans</u>fer

_____   _____   _____

b claustro<u>phobia</u>

_____   _____   _____

c archae<u>ology</u>

_____   _____   _____

d <u>super</u>natural

_____   _____   _____

e <u>aero</u>dynamic

_____   _____   _____

Exploring Further …

Choose a prefix or suffix from the fish to complete the words. Use each only once.

tele   **trans**   **bi**   **micro**   **logy**   **aero**

_____ centenary   zoo _____

_____ vision   _____ scope

_____ port   _____ plane

Now soar to pages 44–45 to record what you have learned in your explorer's logbook

Quick test

Now try these questions. Give yourself 1 mark for every correct answer – but only if you answer each part of the question correctly.

1   What word with the prefix **trans**- means 'see-through'? _____

2   Circle the correct spelling of the underlined words:
    She was given good advise/advice for practicing/practising her spellings.

3   Insert prefixes that will change the adjectives in this sentence into negative adjectives:

    The _____ adequate researcher's data was _____ complete.

4   Circle the correct spelling of the underlined words:
    I was warn/worn out from too/to much lifting of such heavy waits/weights.

5   Join the words using a hyphen to make adjectives:

    good   haired   _____

    custom   looking   _____

    wide   built   _____

    dark   eyed   _____

6   Make both an adjective and an adverb from the following nouns:

	adjective	adverb
misery		
allowance		
understanding		
desire		

7   Use the **ough** letter string to spell these sentences correctly:

    I thawt the coff was bad enuff, so I bawt the coff medicine. Luckily, I had just enuff money!

    _____

    _____

8   Add **cial** or **tial** to these words to form adjectives, making necessary spelling changes:

    commerce   _____   influence   _____

9   Turn these nouns into adjectives ending **ent** or **ant**:

    independence _____   importance _____

10 Make both an adverb and an adjective from the following nouns:

	adverb	adjective
terror		
horror		
sense		
vision		

11 Add either the suffix **ance** or **ence** to make nouns from the following verbs:

appear   _____   insist   _____

interfere   _____   endure   _____

12 Turn these words into negative versions by adding the prefix **dis** or **mis**:

similar   _____   led   _____

understanding   _____   guided   _____

13 Use the suffixes **ise**, **ify**, **ate** or **en** to make verbs from these words:

short   _____   priority   _____

sign   _____   indication _____

14 Underline the silent letters in the words below:

gnome   foreign

knotted   hour

15 Add both the suffixes **ing** and **ed** to each of these words:

simplify   _____   _____

dignify   _____   _____

16 Add either the prefix **il** or **ir** to the following words:

responsible   _____   legible   _____

logical   _____   respective   _____

17 The following anagrams contain the suffixes **cious** and **tious**. Unravel them to find what they really are:

pus ecori   _____   susus cio pi   _____

ucit usa o   _____   us oi nocsic net   _____

18 Add the suffixes **ing**, or, **er** to make nouns from these infinitives:

to suffer   _____   _____

to attack   _____   _____

19 Add the suffixes **ed**, **ing**, **ence** to each of these words to make new words:

refer   _____   _____   _____

infer   _____   _____   _____

20 Some of the following words are spelled incorrectly; find which ones they are and rewrite them correctly:

receipt   cieling   yeild   peice   deceive   sieze   nieghbour   field   veins

_____

_____

Explorer's Logbook

Tick off the topics as you complete them and then colour in the star.

How do you feel?
- Needs practice
- Nearly there
- Got it!

Words ending fer ☐

Suffixes ible and ibly ☐

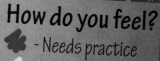

Rules: *i* before *e* ☐

Suffixes cious or tious? ☐

Suffixes able and ably ☐

Suffixes ent and ant ☐

Suffixes ence and ance ☐

Using hyphens ☐

Suffixes cial and tial ☐

Making nouns ☐

Silent letters ☐

Making verbs ☐

Changing y to i ☐

Prefixes dis and mis ☐

Prefixes im and in ☐

Prefixes il and ir ☐

Ough letter strings ☐

Homophones and homonyms ☐

Super-tricky homophones ☐

Latin and Greek ☐

Answers

Pages 2–3
Task 1
a dependable **b** comfortable
c allowable **d** acceptable
Appropriate sentences with the words used in context are acceptable.
Task 2
a changeable **b** noticeable **c** lovable
d desirable **e** breathable
Task 3
a considerably **b** understandably
c advisably **d** reasonably **e** reliably
Exploring Further
a considerably **b** understandably
c reliable **d** replaceable

Pages 4–5
Task 1
a horrible **b** terrible **c** sensible
d reversible **e** audible
Task 2
a sensibly **b** forcibly **c** visibly
d divisibly **e** irresistibly
Task 3
Any appropriate sentences using five of the words from Tasks 1 and 2 are acceptable.
Exploring Further
ACCESSIBLE   LEGIBLY
SENSIBLY   RESPONSIBLY
COLLAPSIBLE

Pages 6–7
Task 1
a social **b** glacial
c facial **d** beneficial
Task 2
a glacial **b** social
c beneficial **d** facial
Task 3
a official **d** commercial
b residential **e** influential
c essential **f** torrential
Exploring Further

I	T	A	P	S	L	A	I	C	A	R
A	R	L	R	K	O	S	N	D	E	A
R	A	A	E	O	M	C	F	S	A	C
T	O	I	M	A	R	T	I	A	L	I
I	A	T	A	C	A	D	N	A	D	L
F	S	A	R	I	E	D	A	H	L	A
I	B	P	O	N	L	E	N	P	E	I
C	U	S	T	A	G	O	C	E	I	C
I	N	I	T	I	A	L	I	H	C	A
A	A	R	E	S	H	C	A	W	N	L
L	A	I	T	R	A	P	L	P	U	G

Pages 8–9
Task 1
a vicious **b** malicious **c** spacious
d officious **e** avaricious **f** gracious
g suspicious **h** ferocious
Task 2
a ambitious **b** infectious **c** nutritious
d conscientious **e** fictitious
Task 3
a fractious — unruly, irritable
b conscious — aware
c pretentious — self-important
d tenacious — determined
e avaricious — greedy
Exploring Further
a nutritious **b** conscious **c** ambitious
d pretentious **e** fractious

Pages 10–11
Task 1
a hesitance **b** tolerance **c** obedience
d innocence **e** dominance **f** defence
Task 2
a clearance **b** reassurance **c** compliance
d endurance **e** appliance **f** guidance
Task 3
a interference **b** preference **c** adherence
d inference **e** transference **f** conference
Exploring Further
a perseverance **b** absence **c** reliance
d insistence **e** existence

Pages 12–13
Task 1
a contestant **b** assistant
c resident **d** accountant **e** applicant
Task 2
a tolerant **b** independent
c hesitant **d** obedient
Task 3
a ascent **b** fluency **c** dominant
Task 4
a transparency **b** pregnancy
c truancy **d** buoyancy
Exploring Further
a N **b** A **c** N **d** N **e** A

Pages 14–15
Task 1

	-ed	-ing	-ence
refer	referred	referring	reference
prefer	preferred	preferring	preference
infer	inferred	inferring	inference
transfer	transferred	transferring	transference

Task 2
a transferred or referred **b** referral
c preference **d** inferred
Task 3
a deference **b** sufferance **c** offering **d** proffering
e difference **f** conference

Exploring Further
Dictionary definitions should be given.

Pages 16–17
Task 1

a co-operate   **b** re-sort   **c** de-icer
d re-enter   **e** co-own   **f** re-cover
g co-worker   **h** re-sent

Task 2

a self-employed   **b** sugar-free   **c** bad-tempered
d part-time   **e** open-mouthed   **f** blonde-haired

Task 3

a custom-built
b up-to-date
c quick-thinking

Exploring Further
Answers will vary. Some examples include:

accident/injury	-	**prone**
sport/football/music	-	**mad**
thick/fair/dark	-	**skinned**
quick/slow/sharp	-	**thinking**

Pages 18–19
Task 1

a field   **b** piece   **c** mischief   **d** brief

Task 2

a received   **b** fierce   **c** believe   **d** weighed

Task 3

a weight   **b** veins   **c** caffeine   **d** neighbour   **e** neigh
f leisure   **g** eighth

Exploring Further
Across

3. seized
4. protein
6. height
7. conceive

Down

1. beige
2. weird
3. sufficient
5. shield

Pages 20–21
Task 1

a drought   **b** through   **c** brought
d enough   **e** thorough

Task 2

Appropriate sentences with all words spelled correctly and used in context.

Task 3

Examples: ought, bought, nought, fought, sought, brought

Exploring Further
a borough   **b** through   **c** dough   **d** ought

Pages 22–23
Task 1

a gnarl   **b** psychology   **c** Wednesday
d wreckage   **e** succumb   **f** knitting

Task 2

Accept any five suitable words, e.g. knit.

Task 3

Accept any five suitable words, e.g. wreck.

Task 4

a island   **b** numb   **c** wrestle
d silhouette   **e** scientists

Exploring Further
G: sign, high, light, reign
D: handkerchief, adjust, edge, bridge
N: autumn, column, condemn, solemn
P: corps, coup, raspberry, cupboard

Pages 24–25
Task 1

a wail   **b** serial   **c** mourning
d wright/write/rite   **e** scene   **f** pane

Task 2

a toad/towed   **b** profit/prophet
c warn/worn   **d** raise/rays/raze
e pores/pours   **f** flex/flecks

Task 3

a We watched as the Arctic hare ate the twigs and roots of the tree.
b A male Arctic hare likes to catch the attention of the female by boxing his competitors.
c A fully-grown Arctic hare can be 5.5kg in weight.
d After the attack by the bear, the Arctic hare was left with bleeding paws.
e It didn't seem fair that the Arctic hare had to die.

Exploring Further
Homophone game.

Pages 26–27
Task 1

a affect   **b** practice   **c** advice
d licence

Task 2

a farther   **b** guest   **c** complimented

Task 3

Accept any grammatically correct sentences containing the homophones.

Exploring Further
a except   **b** allusion   **c** Briton   **d** device

Pages 28–29
Task 1

a disappoint   **b** misrepresent   **c** disfigure
d disagree   **e** misunderstanding   **f** misguided
g disconnect   **h** dishonest

Task 2

a misspell   **b** dishonest   **c** misfortune
d mislaid   **e** disloyal

Task 3

a misled   **b** disagree   **c** disappointed
d mislaid   **e** dissimilar

Exploring Further
Answers will vary. Accept any appropriate passage with words used in context.

Pages 30–31
Task 1

a impolite   **b** immobile   **c** indecent
d incapable   **e** improbable   **f** inoffensive

Task 2

a inability   **b** impersonal   **c** immodest
d invalid   **e** impossible

Task 3

a impatient   **b** inadequate   **c** incomplete
d immobile   **e** inaccurate

Exploring Further
Answers will vary. Accept any appropriate sentences using the words given in the correct context.

Pages 32–33
Task 1

a illiterate   **b** irregular   **c** illegitimate
d illegible   **e** irreparable   **f** irreversible
g irrelevant

Task 2
a irresponsible b illogical c illegal d irrespective
Task 3
a illegal b illiterate c irrational d irrelevant
Exploring Further
a irresistible b illiterate c irrational d illogical

Pages 34–35
Task 1
a situation
b building/builder
c education/educator
d creation/creator
e gardening/gardener
f suggestion
g invention/inventor
h invitation
Task 2
a attacker b hearing c adviser d hunters
Task 3
a assistant/assistance
b relative/relativity/relevance/relation
c government/governance/governing
d publicity/publication
Exploring Further

Infinitive	Noun (1)	Noun (2)
To police	policing	police
To investigate	investigator	investigation
To cook	cook	cooker
To nurse	nursing	nurse
To prey	predator	prey

Pages 36–37
Task 1
a identify b indicate c magnify
d lengthen e prioritise
Task 2
a apologise b advertise c sympathise
d improvise e classify f modify
g pacify h horrify
Task 3
a apologise b clarify c customise
d strengthen e hesitate
Exploring Further
a hyphenate b fossilise c solidify d broaden
Accept appropriate sentences with words used in context.

Pages 38–39
Task 1
a laziness/lazier/laziest/lazily
b naughtiness/naughtier/naughtiest/naughtily
c prettiness/prettier/prettiest/prettily
d silliness/sillier/silliest/sillily
e stealthiness/stealthier/stealthiest/stealthily
Task 2
a multiplying/multiplied
b varying/varied
c certifying/certified
d accompanying/accompanied
e obeying/obeyed
Task 3
a jolliest b variety c identification d justification
Exploring Further
Answers will vary. Examples include:
application/applicant/applying/applied
satisfaction/satisfying/satisfied
reliant/relying/relied

Pages 40–41
Task 1
a a motor car (self-propelled)
b a book you write about yourself
c a signature, in one's own handwriting
auto means self
Task 2
Accept appropriate sentences with words used in context.
Task 3
Answers will vary.
Exploring Further
bicentenary, television, transport, zoology, microscope, aeroplane

Answers to Quick Test
1 transparent
2 advice, practising
3 inadequate, incomplete
4 worn, too, weights
5 good-looking, custom-built, wide-eyed, dark-haired
6

	adjective	adverb
misery	miserable	miserably
allowance	allowable	allowably
understanding	understandable	understandably
desire	desirable	desirably

7 I thought the cough was bad enough so I bought the cough medicine. Luckily I had just enough money!
8 commercial, influential
9 independent, important
10

	adverb	adjective
terror	terribly	terrible
horror	horribly	horrible
sense	sensibly	sensible
vision	visibly	visible

11 appearance, interference, insistence, endurance
12 dissimilar, misunderstanding, misled, misguided
13 shorten, signify, prioritise, indicate
14 gnome, knotted, foreign, hour
15 simplifying, simplified; dignifying, dignified
16 irresponsible, illogical, illegible, irrespective
17 precious, cautious, suspicious, conscientious
18 suffering, sufferer, attacker, attacking
19 referred, referring, reference; inferred, inferring, inference
20 Correct words: receipt, deceive, field, veins
Correct spelling of incorrect words: ceiling, yield, piece, seize, neighbour